# My Little Lore of Light Coloring Book

## Karima Sperling

## Note to the Children

You will notice that the faces in this book are left empty. There is a reason for this. The light of Muhammad (sas) shone so brightly on the faces of Allah's Prophets that their beauty was unlike that of other people. When people looked at the faces of their Prophets they saw light and love and everything that was most beautiful. We cannot picture this light or love on paper. We cannot draw faces that to everyone will look the most beautiful. So we leave the faces without features and let our imaginations picture them in our minds. In this way we will show our respect for the finest of Allah's creation and keep the light and the love for His Prophets safe in our hearts.

Other Titles By This Author:

My Little Lore of Light
The Light of Muhammad
Links of Light: The Golden Chain
The Story of Moses
Who Are You? A Book of Very Serious Questions
The Animals of Paradise
The Animals of Paradise: Coloring Book
Every Day A Thousand Times

Printed in the United States of America ISBN 978-0-9913003-5-8

Little Bird Books littlebirdbooksink@gmail.com

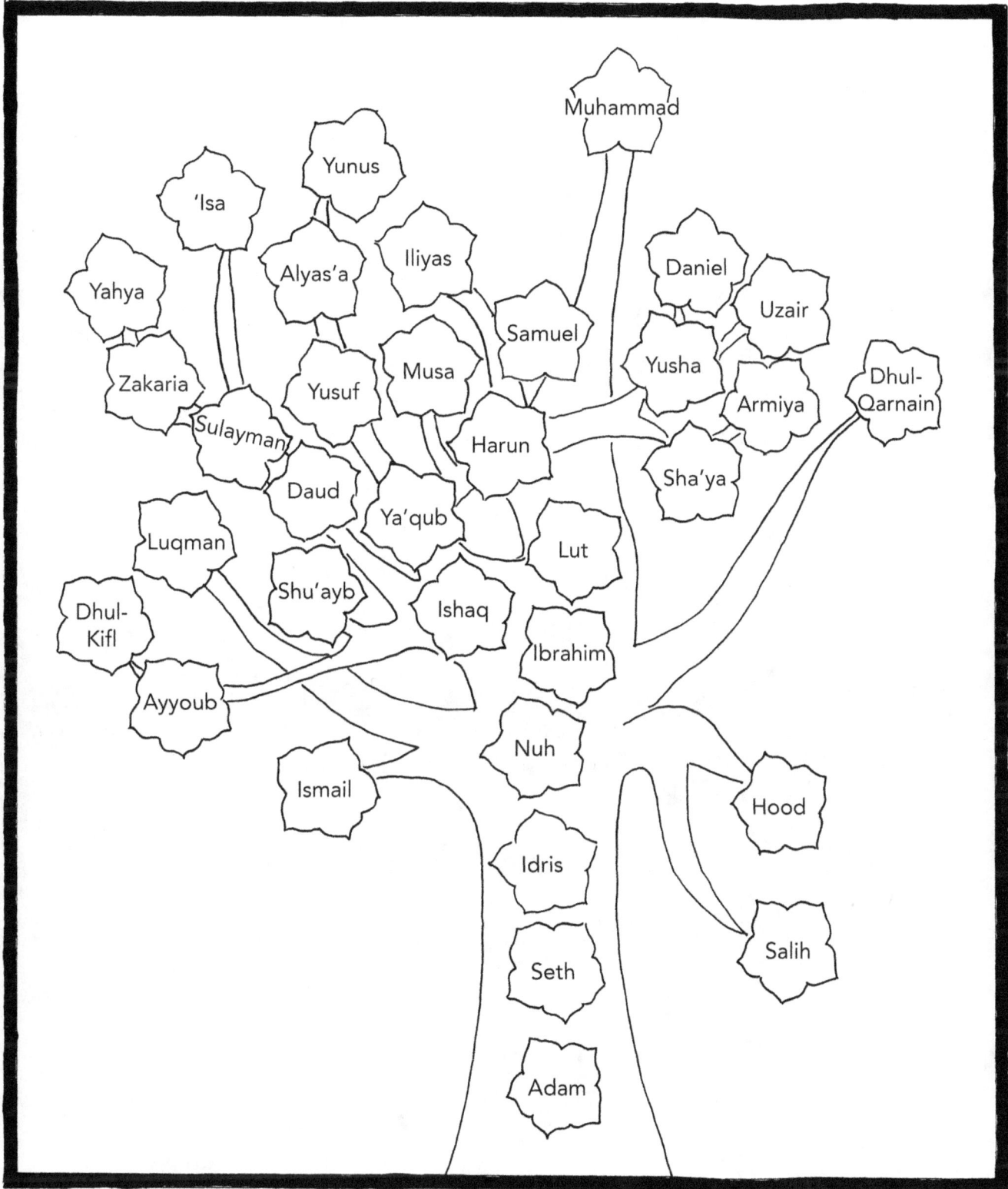

Muhammad · 'Isa · Yunus · Yahya · Iliyas · Alyas'a · Daniel · Uzair · Zakaria · Samuel · Musa · Yusuf · Yusha · Armiya · Dhul-Qarnain · Sulayman · Harun · Sha'ya · Daud · Ya'qub · Lut · Luqman · Shu'ayb · Ishaq · Dhul-Kifl · Ibrahim · Ayyoub · Nuh · Hood · Ismail · Idris · Seth · Salih · Adam

# Tree of Prophets

# Adam alayhi s-salam

"Your Lord said to the angels, I am going to put My deputy on the Earth." (2:30)

# Seth alayhi s-salam

"Did I not take a promise from you, O Children of Adam ..." (36:60)

# Idris alayhi s-salam

"And remember Idris in the book, he was a man of truth and a prophet." (19:56)

# Nuh alayhi s-salam

"And it moved on with them into waves that were like mountains." (11:42)

# Hood alayhi s-salam

"They said, 'This is a cloud bringing us rain.' No it is...a wind in which is painful punishment, destroying everything by the command of its Lord." (46:24-25)

## Salih alayhi s-salam

"This is Allah's she-camel - a sign for you. So leave her alone to pasture in Allah's earth, and do her no harm." (7:73)

# Ibrahim alayhi s-salam

"We (Allah) said, 'O fire, be coolness and peace for Ibrahim.'" (21:69)

# Ismail alayhi s-salam

"O my father, do as you are commanded; if Allah please you will find me patient." (37:102)

## Lut alayhi s-salam

"We (Allah) turned them upside down and rained on them stones... marked by your Lord with names." (11:82-83)

## Ishaq alayhi s-salam

"We (Allah) give you good news of a boy possessing knowledge." (15:53)

# Ya'qub alayhi s-salam

"And he turned away from them and said: Oh my sorrow for Yusuf." (12:84)

# Yusuf alayhi s-salam

"He (Yusuf) said, 'No blame on you this day. May Allah forgive you.'" (12:92)

# Ayyoub alayhi s-salam

"Stamp with your foot. Here is cool water to wash with and to drink." (38:42)

# Dhul-Kifl alayhi s-salam

"And remember Ismail and Alyasa' and Dhul-Kifl and they were all of the best ones." (38:48)

# Shu'ayb alayhi s-salam

"Those who called Shu'ayb a liar, they were the losers." (7:92)

## Musa alayhi s-salam

"Place him into an ark, then put it into the river. The river will bring it to shore." (20:39)

Harun alayhi s-salam

"Then We sent Musa and his brother Harun with Our signs and a clear authority." (23:45)

# Yusha alayhi s-salam

"O my people enter the Holy Land which Allah has promised you." (5:21)

# Samuel alayhi s-salam

"And their prophet said to them, 'Surely Allah has raised Talut to be king over you.'" (2:247)

# Daud alayhi s-salam

"We (Allah) caused the hills and the birds to join Daud in celebrating Our praises." (21:79)

# Luqman alayhi s-salam

"And certainly We gave Luqman wisdom." (31:12)

# Sulayman alayhi s-salam

"Around Sulayman were gathered his companies of Jinn, men and birds." (27:17)

Iliyas alayhi s-salam

"And Zakariya and Yahya and 'Isa and Iliyas: all of them are among the righteous." (6:85)

# Alyas'a alayhi s-salam

"And Ismail and Alyas'a and Yunus and Lut: and all of them we favored above the nations."
(6:86)

# Yunus alayhi s-salam

"Then the big fish did swallow him." (37:142)

## Sha'ya alayhi s-salam

"Whenever a messenger came to you with what you did not like you were arrogant. Some you called liars and others you killed. (2:87)

## Armiya alayhi s-salam

"And there never was a people who did not have among them a person to warn them." (35:24)

## Daniel alayhi s-salam

"Ibrahim and Ismail prayed...our Lord raise up from among them (our descendants) a messenger to recite to them Your signs, and teach them the book and wisdom and purify them." (2:129)

# Uzair alayhi s-salam

"He (Allah) gives life to the dead and He is possessor of power over all things." (42:9)

# Dhul-Qarnain alayhi s-salam

"Truly We gave him power in the earth and the means for all things." (18:84)

# Zakaria alayhi s-salam

"Whenever Zakaria entered her place of prayer (mihrab) he found food with her." (3:37)

# Yahya alayhi s-salam

"And We granted him wisdom as a child, and kind-heartedness from Us and purity." (19:12-13)

And We granted him ... a child, and kind ... [19:12-13]

## 'Isa alayhi s-salam

"'Isa son of Maryam said: O Allah, our Lord, send down to us a table (of food) from heaven."
(5:114)

# Muhammad
## sall Allahu alayhi wa sallam

"Glory be to Him who carried His servant by night from the sacred mosque to the farthest mosque...that We might show him of Our signs." (17:1)

# Muhammad
# sall Allahu alayhi wa sallam
"And We sent you as a mercy to all the worlds." (21:107)

www.ingramcontent.com/pod-product-compliance
Lightning Source LLC
Chambersburg PA
CBHW080527030426
42337CB00023B/4661